AUTHENTIC LEADER

BILL DONAHUE

IVP Connect

InterVarsity Press
Downers Grove, Illinois

Inter-Varsity Press
Leicester, England

InterVarsity Press, USA
P.O. Box 1400, Downers Grove, IL 60515-1426, USA
World Wide Web: www.ivpress.com
E-mail: mail@ivpress.com

Inter-Varsity Press, England
38 De Montfort Street, Leicester LE1 7GP, England
Website: www.ivpbooks.com
E-mail: ivp@ivp-editorial.co.uk

InterVarsity Press®, USA, is the book-publishing division of InterVarsity Christian Fellowship/USA®, a student movement active on campus at hundreds of universities, colleges and schools of nursing in the United States of America, and a member movement of the International Fellowship of Evangelical Students. For information about local and regional activities, write Public Relations Dept., InterVarsity Christian Fellowship/USA, 6400 Schroeder Rd., P.O. Box 7895, Madison, WI 53707-7895, or visit the IVCF website at <www.intervarsity.org>.

Inter-Varsity Press, England, is the publishing division of the Universities and Colleges Christian Fellowship (formerly the Inter-Varsity Fellowship), a student movement linking Christian Unions in universities and colleges throughout Great Britain, and a member movement of the International Fellowship of Evangelical Students. For information about local and national activities write to UCCF, 38 De Montfort Street, Leicester LE1 7GP, email us at email@uccf.org.uk, or visit the UCCF website at www.uccf.org.uk.

All Scripture quotations, unless otherwise indicated, are taken from the Holy Bible, New International Version®. NIV®. Copyright © 1973, 1978, 1984 by International Bible Society. Used by permission of Zondervan Publishing House. Distributed in the U.K. by permission of Hodder and Stoughton Ltd. All rights reserved. "NIV" is a registered trademark of International Bible Society. UK trademark number 1448790.

Design: Cindy Kiple

Images: Lisa Thompson/Getty Images

USA ISBNs   0-8308-2155-4
            978-0-8308-2155-6

UK ISBNs   1-84474-112-5
            978-1-84474-112-0

Printed in the United States of America ∞

| P | 19 | 18 | 17 | 16 | 15 | 14 | 13 | 12 | 11 | 10 | 9 | 8 | 7 | 6 | 5 | 4 | 3 | 2 | 1 |
| Y | 19 | 18 | 17 | 16 | 15 | 14 | 13 | 12 | 11 | 10 | 09 | 08 | 07 | 06 | 05 | | | | |

CONTENTS

BEFORE YOU BEGIN

The Jesus 101 series is designed to help you respond to Jesus as you encounter him in the stories and teachings of the Bible, particularly the Gospel accounts of the New Testament. The "101" designation does not mean "simple"; it means "initial." You probably took introductory-level courses in high school or at a university, like Economics 101 or Biology 101. Each was an initial course, a first encounter with the teachings and principles of the subject matter. I had my first encounter with economic theory in Econ 101, but it was not necessarily simple or always easy (at least not for me!).

Jesus 101 may be the first time you looked closely at Jesus. For the first time you will encounter his grace and love, be exposed to his passion and mission, and get a firsthand look at the way he connects with people like you and me. Or perhaps, like me, you have been a Christian many years. In that case you will encounter Jesus for the first time all over again. Often when I read a biblical account of an event in Jesus' life, even if the text is very familiar to me, I am amazed at a new insight or a fresh, personal connection with Jesus I hadn't experienced before.

I believe Jesus 101 will challenge your thinking and stir your soul regardless of how far along the spiritual pathway you might be. After all, Jesus is anything but dull: he tended to shake up the world of everyone who interacted with him. Sometimes people sought him out; often he surprised them. In every case, he challenged them, evoking a reaction they could hardly ignore.

There are many ways we might encounter Jesus. In this series we will focus on eight. You will come face to face with Jesus as

- Provocative Teacher
- Sacred Friend
- Extreme Forgiver
- Authentic Leader
- Truthful Revealer
- Compassionate Healer
- Relentless Lover
- Supreme Conqueror

☐ HOW THESE GUIDES ARE PUT TOGETHER

In each of the discussion guides you will find material for six group meetings, though feel free to use as many meetings as necessary to cover the material. That is up to you. Each group will find its way. The important thing is to encounter and connect with Christ, listen to what he is saying, watch what he is doing—and then personalize that encounter individually and as a group.

The material is designed to help you engage with one another, with the Bible and with the person of Jesus. The experiences below are designed to guide you along when you come together as a group.

Gathering to Listen

This short section orients you to the material by using an illustration, a quote or a text that raises probing questions, makes provocative assumptions or statements, or evokes interpersonal tension or thoughtfulness. It may just make you laugh. It sets the tone for the dialogue you will be having together. Take a moment here to connect with one another and focus your attention on the reading. Listen carefully as thoughts and emotions are stirred.

After the reading, you will have an opportunity to respond in some way. What are your first impressions, your assumptions, disagreements, feelings? What comes to mind as you read this?

Encountering Jesus

Here you meet Jesus as he is described in the Bible text. You will encounter his teachings, his personal style and his encounters with people much like you. This section will invite your observations, questions and initial reactions to what Jesus is saying and doing.

Joining the Conversation

A series of group questions and interactions will encourage your little community to engage with one another about the person and story of Jesus. Here you will remain for a few moments in the company of Jesus and of one another. This section may pose a question about your group or ask you to engage in an exercise or interaction with one another. The goal is to discover a sense of community as you question and discover what God is doing.

Connecting Our Stories

Here you are invited to connect your story (life, issues, questions, challenges) with Jesus' story (his teaching, character and actions). We look at our background and history, the things that encourage or disappoint us. We seek to discover what God is doing in our life and the lives of others, and we develop a sense of belonging and understanding.

Finding Our Way

A final section of comments and questions invites you to investigate next steps for your spiritual journey as a group and personally. It will evoke and prompt further action, decisions or conversations in response to what was discovered and discussed. You will prompt one another to listen to God more deeply, take relational risks and invite God's work in your group and in the community around you.

Praying Together

God's Holy Spirit is eager to teach you! Remember that learning is not just a mental activity; it involves relationship and action. One educator suggests that all learning is the result of failed expectations. We hope, then, that at some point your own expectations will fail, that you will be ambushed by the truth and stumble into new and unfamiliar territory that startles you into new ways of thinking about God and relating to him through Christ. And so prayer—talking and listening to God—is a vital part of the Jesus 101 journey.

If you are seeking to discover Jesus for the first time, your prayer can be a very simple expression of your thoughts and questions to God. It may include emotions like anger, frustration, joy or wonder. If you already have an intimate, conversational relationship with God, your prayer will reflect the deepest longings and desires of your soul. Prayer is an integral part of the spiritual life, and small groups are a great place to explore it.

☐ HOW DO I PREPARE?

No preparation is required! Reading the Bible text ahead of time, if you can, will provide an overview of what lies ahead and will give you an opportunity to reflect on the Bible passages. But you will not feel out of the loop or penalized in some way if you do not get to it. This material is designed for *group* discovery and interaction. A sense of team and community develops and excitement grows as you explore the material together. In contrast to merely discussing what everyone has already discovered prior to the meeting, "discovery in the moment" evokes a sense of shared adventure.

If you want homework, do that after each session. Decide how you might face your week, your job, your relationships and family in light of what you have just discovered about Jesus.

☐ A FINAL NOTE

These studies are based on the book *In the Company of Jesus*. It is not required that you read the book to do any Jesus 101 study—each stands alone. But you might consider reading the parallel sections of the book to enrich your experience between small group meetings. The major sections of the book take up the same eight ways that we encounter Jesus in the Jesus 101 guides. So the eight guides mirror the book in structure and themes, but the material in the book is not identical to that of the guides.

Jesus 101 probes more deeply into the subject matter, whereas *In the Company of Jesus* is designed for devotional and contemplative reading and prayer. It is filled with stories and anecdotes to inspire and motivate you in your relationship with Christ.

I pray and hope that you enjoy this adventure as you draw truth from the Word of God for personal transformation, group growth and living out God's purposes in the world!

INTRODUCTION

THE AUTHENTIC LEADER

"God save us from know-it-all leaders," writes Dave Fleming. "God save us from *becoming* know-it-all leaders" ("Leadership Wisdom from Unlikely Voices," *Rev.,* Sept.-Oct. 2004). Such leaders rarely grow, becoming predictable and stifling the growth of others in the community they lead. Fleming contends that they have an overly futuristic view of leadership: they seem to always be looking toward new ideas and theories and to pay little attention to the past. They have little regard for past wisdom and believe that only in the future will they discover what they need for building their organization.

Every endeavor needs fresh voices. Without innovation and creativity, any group or team can begin to embrace the status quo and soon find itself left behind. But, as Fleming argues, some important "innovations" come from the past. Leaders do well to consult their predecessors—to seek ancient wisdom—for help in guiding people into the future.

"When we ignore the past," he warns, "we relegate leadership to the surface of cultural change rather than to the domain of human experience that transcends epochs and eras." Authentic leaders—real leaders, honest leaders—know that they stand on the shoulders of others. Guided by a spirit of humility, authentic leaders recognize that they need the insights and counsel of others.

Jesus understood this. The Bible tells us that as a youth, he grew in wisdom even as he grew in stature. As an itinerant teacher, he was quick to tell his followers that he came to fulfill the Law and the Prophets, not to ignore and abolish the teachings of the past. Yes, his teaching was fresh and enlightening, like replacing a 40-watt bulb with a flood light!

We have in Jesus Christ an authentic leader, one who is truthful and honest about the past, connects to the present and points his followers to a future that builds on both. His leadership is demanding and challenging, yet grace filled and Spirit led. He is Lord and Master, worthy of our devotion. And he is a leader worth following. He expects us to follow him faithfully and to give him our best effort, yet he is eager to restore us when we fail and reward us when we obey.

As the Son of God, Jesus knew it all—but he never sounded like a know-it-all leader. His is a life worth following and a leadership worth emulating.

ONE

RELEASES OUR STRENGTHS

He appointed the twelve,
that he might send them out to preach.

☐ **GATHERING TO LISTEN**

Sergeant Sobol was responsible for training Easy Company, a section of the U.S. Army's elite Airborne paratrooper force during World War II. The television series and book *Band of Brothers* document the heroic acts of Easy Company and Sobol's training methods. His tactics often appeared cruel and unorthodox to new recruits. He wanted the best-equipped and best-conditioned fighting force possible, but sometimes he went too far.

On one occasion he decided to offer the men an afternoon of rest after several weeks of nonstop training and harassment. He ordered a special lunch for them that day—a spaghetti meal that was a welcome alternative to the tasteless army chow they had been eating. Naturally, they were elated and consumed multiple helpings of the unexpected repast.

Suddenly, as the meal was ending, Sobol burst into the dining hall and announced that the free afternoon was canceled. "Follow me," he yelled.

"We are running Curahee!" Curahee was a hill the men were forced to run regularly—a grueling three miles up and three miles down. The men were filled with rage as they realized Sobol had deliberately tricked them into filling their stomachs before making the demanding six-mile run in the afternoon heat. You can imagine what happened along the way as the men struggled to complete the task on a full stomach.

Eventually Sobol did produce a stellar unit in the Airborne, but it came at a high price. His abusive tactics and disdain for his men demoralized them. Instead of releasing their strengths, he had actually undermined them, pushing the young soldiers almost to the point of mutiny. As a result, his superiors transferred his command to another officer, never allowing Sobol to take Easy Company into battle.

- Without naming anyone in particular, have you ever found that your strengths were ignored or overlooked by a leader? What was it like?

☐ ENCOUNTERING JESUS

Jesus wanted to see his followers develop and succeed in the ministry he was giving them. If they trusted him and used the power he was giving them, they would see amazing results.

Read Luke 9:1-6.

1. It is frustrating to be given responsibility without authority or adequate resources. In light of the task Jesus gives the Twelve, what kind of power and authority is Jesus giving his inner circle?

2. Jesus desires to release the strengths of his disciples, but he wants them to understand the real source of their power. As you read verse 3, what is he trying to produce in them, and why is this essential to their success?

3. What does the instruction in verse 5 (see also Matthew 10:14) reveal about the character, message and authority of Jesus?

☐ **JOINING THE CONVERSATION**

4. Christ followers are given power and authority to act and live in the name of Jesus (Matthew 28:18-20 also declares this). God is eager to release your strength, but only after you learn dependence on him. How aware are you of the power and authority God has provided, and how does this affect your daily life?

5. Not everyone received Jesus or his message. How does the possibility of rejection make you feel as you consider following the ways of Jesus?

6. In this case, the disciples experience great blessing and powerful re-
    sults. How does this compare with what you experience?

☐ **CONNECTING OUR STORIES**

7. Think of some areas of life in which you need the power of God these
    days, and how you need God's power to help you meet that need or
    opportunity.

My Need	God's Power Released

8. According to 1 Corinthians 12 and Romans 12, God has given us
    gifts. But these gifts are to be used in his power. Which of the follow-
    ing is your response to God's gifts and power, and why?

    • I tend to act without considering God at all.

    • I am aware that God gives me power, but I'm not sure I ever really
    use it.

    • When I am facing a major decisions or problem, I seek God's
    power.

    • I am very aware of the authority and power I have in Christ, and I
    rely on that power often.

9. What fears or obstacles can keep you from relying on the power of Jesus more regularly?

☐ **FINDING OUR WAY**

10. Our strengths are made perfect in weakness, according to Paul in 2 Corinthians. This is the paradox of Christianity: we have strengths that God wants to release, but we must depend on his power to release them in ways that further God's purposes. How can we encourage one another to draw on God's power?

☐ **PRAYING TOGETHER**

Are you willing to put all your strengths at the disposal of Christ in order to experience his power? He is eager to use them because he has given you many gifts, talents and experiences. As you submit to his leadership, you will find that he is more than willing to use you—in ways that you could never have envisioned on your own.

Pray that God will show you his power. Remember that you have been given authority—not to wield for selfish ambition but to represent Jesus.

TWO

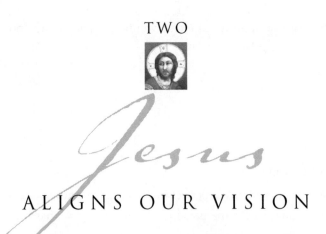

ALIGNS OUR VISION

*Why do you look at the speck of sawdust in your brother's eye
and pay no attention to the plank in your own eye?*

☐ GATHERING TO LISTEN

Ever look at one of those books that ask you to identify specific objects
in the picture? On the page you see a conglomeration of objects—hundreds of them—but you must locate five or six specific items. You might
be told to find a pen, a paper clip, a blue button, a small watch and a red
ball. Sounds simple, except the photograph includes a seemingly endless
array of colors, shapes and gadgets.

For example, you are asked to find a white bird. You scour every
square inch of the photo, becoming more frustrated as time moves on.
You see tiny cars, spools of thread, gears, paper dolls, small stuffed ani-
mals, shoelaces, bottle tops and an assortment of things you'd find in
your junk drawer. But no white bird.

Just when you are about to give up, your eight-year-old child walks
into the room and takes a look. "I see the bird!" she yells, pointing at
the page.

"Where?" you ask.

"Everywhere!" she exclaims. Indeed. All the little objects in the photo lie on a large piece of white paper—cleverly cut out in the shape of a bird. You thought the bird was on the pile, but the pile was on the bird.

- Have you ever had a similar experience? If so, describe it.
- Why is it that we are sometimes blind to the obvious?

☐ **ENCOUNTERING JESUS**

Jesus was confronted with blind people all the time—except their eyesight was just fine. They had vision problems that could not have been corrected with glasses or contact lenses or even laser surgery. Ironically, their vision problem had nothing to do with their eyes.

Read Matthew 7:1-5.

1. Jesus confronts his followers about judging others. What is the difference between this kind of judging and the judging he asks people to do in John 7:21-24?

2. What is both humorous and human about the illustration Jesus uses in verses 3-5?

3. What might Jesus be trying to protect his disciples from?

Why is this issue so important to their mission in the world?

☐ JOINING THE CONVERSATION

4. List the characteristics of a person you experience as judgmental.

Might others use any of these words to describe you?

5. Why do we tend to be eager to pass judgment on others?

6. What is it about the plank in your own eye that makes it difficult to see?

□ **Connecting Our Stories**

7. What would you like to change about the way you respond to people's failures and mistakes?

What needs to happen in your heart?

8. How might others view Christians if church members really followed the teaching of Jesus here in Matthew 7?

□ **Finding Our Way**

9. In the new community of Jesus followers, we are told to help each other grow and mature. This means doing some "speck removal" by confronting wrongdoing, unhealthy patterns and sin. How can you help each other do that without becoming a finger-pointing, judgmental group?

☐ PRAYING TOGETHER

Take time for personal reflection and confession of judgmental attitudes
and actions. Ask God for a vision exam—ask him to help you see the log
in your own eye. But also ask for courage to help a brother or sister remove the speck in theirs. Jesus is not against speck removal; he is against
hypocritical speck removal. Spiritual growth in community demands that
we help one another grow. But it takes humility, discernment and courage, so pray for these qualities.

THREE

Jesus

DEMANDS OUR DEVOTION

*If anyone would come after me, he must deny himself
and take up his cross daily and follow me.*

☐ **GATHERING TO LISTEN**

There is a difference between demanding leaders and leaders who make
demands. One can never please a demanding leader. Performance stan-
dards are always changing, results are never good enough, and rewards
are seldom given.

I learned the difference between these the hard way. During my first
semester in seminary I worked part time as a football coach for the same
high school team I had played with some nine years earlier. The head
coach asked me to help with the linebackers and defensive ends, posi-
tions I had played in high school and in college. Because of the outstand-
ing record my team had when I played, the players respected me. Each
afternoon I arrived at practice eager to challenge these young men and
shape them into a strong defensive unit.

I pushed the players hard each day, trying to get the best out of them.
After only a few days, however, the head coach called me into his office.

"What are you trying to do to these guys?" he asked. "You keep shouting at them. They'll just get angry at you, and your rapport with them will suffer. Build them up and stop shouting at them so much."

I walked away feeling terrible and determined to salvage my reputation. To a large degree I did, but not fully. The damage was done, and I had learned a hard lesson at the team's expense.

Leaders make demands on followers in order to stretch them. But *how* we make those demands determines whether the result is growth or resentment, a determination to perform or a desire to simply give up. I had been pointing out the errors I saw in the young football players without affirming their achievements. Instead of making challenging demands that they could strive to achieve, I had become demanding and critical. And there is a big difference between the two approaches.

- Reflect on this distinction for a moment. How do you see those differences played out in our world today at work, in politics, business, education or elsewhere?

☐ **ENCOUNTERING JESUS**

Thank goodness Jesus understands the difference between making demands and being an unreasonable and demanding leader.

Read Luke 14:25-35.

1. Why might Jesus address the large crowd this way? (After all, when you are building a ministry or an organization, don't you want lots of followers?)

2. Jesus makes three demands on his would-be followers in this passage. List them and note your initial reaction to these demands.

Demand (verse 26):

My reaction:

Demand (verse 27):

My reaction:

Demand (verse 32):

My reaction:

3. What do you notice about each of Jesus' analogies illustrating the cost of following him? What do they have in common, and how does this link to verse 33?

4. In verses 34-35 Jesus takes it all a step further, pointing to the quality of the life his disciples will lead and the impact they should have. What does saltiness suggest about the character of a follower of Jesus?

☐ JOINING THE CONVERSATION

5. Think about the people listening to Jesus at this point. There were committed disciples, critics, casual followers and curious seekers. How might each group respond to what Jesus is saying?

6. As you reflect on these words of Jesus, try to articulate how you feel about your own spiritual journey. Use any of the statements on page 27 if it helps you put words to your reaction.

- I am fully committed to following Jesus, regardless of the cost to my image or reputation.

- I am a bit fearful because I do not know what "taking up my cross" looks like.

- I am not ready to take any next steps yet because I am still trying to understand why Jesus makes such demands on people.

- I think Jesus is going too far here and is scaring away people who might follow him if they had a chance to get to know him.

- I made the commitment to follow Jesus fully in the past, but I feel I failed him along the way since then. So now I am unsure—will he still want me to follow him after what I have done?

☐ **CONNECTING OUR STORIES**

7. Tell of a time you had to give up something of value (time, money, possessions, relationships) in order to gain something of equal or greater value to you. Was it worth the tradeoff? Would you do it again?

8. Self-denial and self-sacrifice are not popular concepts in our culture. If you are still searching for truth and looking at the life of Jesus, what do his demands feel like to you?

How do Jesus' demands compare to those of other religious systems and teachings?

□ FINDING OUR WAY

9. How difficult would it be for you right now to bring your devotion to Jesus to a higher level? What might it cost you—for example, popularity, money, friends, advancement, time, your pride—to act as "salt" in the world?

10. Discipleship—intentionally following the ways of Jesus—is not intended to be done alone. That would be almost impossible. So how do we help each other meet the demands of following Jesus?

What do we need to remind each other of in order to encourage one another in our faith?

☐ PRAYING TOGETHER

Read Romans 12:9-21, which describes how members of the Jesus community act. Use it as a prayer guide. Do not study it; simply read it slowly as a community. Consider adapting it as your prayer: "Father, help us to have a sincere love for others, to hate things that are evil and to hold on to what is really good. Help us to practice hospitality . . ." and so on through the passage.

FOUR

EXPECTS OUR BEST

Well done, good and faithful servant!

☐ **GATHERING TO LISTEN**

In his excellent book *A Resilient Life,* pastor and speaker Gordon Mac-Donald writes about what he learned in school under the tutelage of track coach Marvin Goldberg. Using athletic training as a metaphor for running the Christian life, MacDonald recounts how Goldberg challenged his runners to excel over time.

> I think you have the potential to be an excellent runner . . . but you have much to learn. If you are to compete for Stony Brook, you're going to have to work hard, discipline yourself. You will have to trust me and follow my instructions. Every day you will have to come to this track and complete the workouts that will be assigned to you. Don't commit to do this if you are not willing to give it everything you have.

Doing our best requires discipline, perseverance and feedback from objective and wise mentors or teachers. Living a faithful life in Christ is no different. It means struggle, training and aligning ourselves with the instructions of the Master Teacher.

- In your present field, what does it take to give your best? (What sacrifices do you make, and what disciplines does it require?)

☐ ENCOUNTERING JESUS

Jesus was a person of discipline and commitment, eager to fulfill with excellence the mission the Father had given him. It makes sense that we who seek to follow him emulate that commitment to do our best in the service of God.

Read Matthew 25:14-30.

This is a parable, a story told by Jesus to help us understand what faithful service looks like and what God expects from his people. Since these workers are entrusted with funds to invest on their boss's behalf, in today's terms it makes sense to think of them as managers.

1. What do you notice about the level of responsibilities given to each man?

2. What do you notice about the response of the owner to each of the managers who produce a good return on the investment?

3. Compare those responses to the one of the manager who hides his talent and does not put it to work.

4. Consider the results and consequences of these managers' actions. What does this tell us about the owner?

☐ JOINING THE CONVERSATION

5. What are some of the striking features of this parable for you?

How does the response of the owner make you feel?

6. Why do you think his response is so forceful? Isn't he being a little harsh toward the cautious manager?

☐ **CONNECTING OUR STORIES**

7. Have you ever disappointed a supervisor or failed to complete a task that your boss gave you to do? What did you discover about yourself?

What did you learn about your boss?

8. If this is a parable about the kingdom of God (about his rule over his creation), what is Jesus trying to get across to us about God and about the life he wants us to lead?

☐ **FINDING OUR WAY**

9. Giving Jesus Christ our best means, in part, using what he has given to us to the best of our ability. We have been entrusted with something. What has he given us? What opportunities lie before us?

How do you plan to use your skills and seize the opportunities?

10. How can we make sure that pleasing God and doing his will does not become a performance-based program we use to earn his favor?

How can we help each other in this regard?

☐ **PRAYING TOGETHER**

Jesus wants us to be wise and responsible when we handle/use his message, his gifts and our abilities. We bring shame to the name of God when we are lazy, fearful or overly cautious and neglect using our resources for his purposes. Pray for strength and wisdom to use God's gifts appropriately without neglect or waste.

FIVE

Jesus

REDEEMS OUR FAILURES

You will all fall away.

☐ GATHERING TO LISTEN

My nine-year-old daughter and I were discussing what we might do for fun one evening. Should we play basketball, play catch, play a board game, watch a short movie or go for a bike ride? She had trouble deciding, but then I had a brainstorm. "Let's make a doghouse for Buddy!" To which she responded, "Cool—that's great."

We needed some materials. Wood was out of the question, because it required using tools that she could not handle. And we didn't have much time: the sun was setting, and it was almost time for her to get ready for bed. We wandered into the garage, found a couple of boxes earmarked for that week's trash and salvaged them for the project.

After some cutting, taping and decorating, we had a doghouse. I thought it was nice and looked okay, but to her it was a castle fit for her favorite stuffed animal, Buddy. Old boxes, assumed to be useless and disposable just a few minutes ago, had provided joy and laughter for a dad and his little girl. A familiar saying came to mind: One person's trash is another one's treasure.

- Tell about a time when you turned trash into treasure or watched your children doing something similar. Or perhaps you considered something useless and obsolete, but someone else found a use for it.

☐ **ENCOUNTERING JESUS**

It is not unusual for us to fail God or realize that we have disappointed him in some way. That's inevitable. We "all fall away" at some point in our relationship with God. For some of us it was many years ago; for others it happens more often than we'd like to admit. As a result we are tempted to believe we have become useless to God; perhaps we should be ignored or discarded. After all, we have done it again—whatever "it" is—and surely this time God is finished with us.

Read Mark 14:29-31, 44-52, 66-72.

1. Peter denies Jesus, and Judas betrays him. The rest of the disciples desert him. Imagine what it would be like to be Jesus at this point—denied, betrayed and deserted. What goes through your mind? What range of emotions might you feel?

2. Jesus encounters his betrayer and those who come to arrest him. What does his response to them in verses 48-49 tell you about Jesus' character and mission?

3. The account of Jesus' arrest found in Luke 22 quotes Jesus saying to his accusers, "Every day I was with you in the temple courts, and you did not lay a hand on me. But this is your hour, when darkness reigns." What is Jesus referring to, and how does this influence his actions (see also Mark 14:50)?

☐ **JOINING THE CONVERSATION**

4. Peter promises to follow Jesus to the end. Like him, in our better moments we think we would never turn on Jesus. But in Peter we see a bit of ourselves. Explain why this is so.

5. Betrayal or desertion in a relationship produces complex fallout. List some of the things you have observed or experienced in the wake of betrayal.

6. What is happening to Peter in Mark 14:71?

How is he different from Judas or even the other disciples?

☐ **CONNECTING OUR STORIES**

7. Have you ever experienced something of what Peter felt—shame and brokenness after disappointing Jesus? Perhaps you denied you knew him or did not stand up for your beliefs under pressure. What did that do to your heart?

8. In John 21 Jesus restores Peter to a place of confidence and leadership. Despite what Peter has done, Jesus gives him the opportunity to express love and devotion for him. What does this tell us about how Jesus views us and our failures?

☐ **FINDING OUR WAY**

9. Jesus restores all of the disciples—except Judas, who has committed suicide—to a place of honor and responsibility. What hope does this give you?

10. When we admit our failures and entrust ourselves to the redeeming work of Jesus, his healing grace and power work in us. How can we grow in confidence that he can redeem those moments and bring healing?

☐ **PRAYING TOGETHER**

Prayers of affirmation may be needed. Pray for and remind one another that failure is not fatal, that God is in the business of redeeming failures. Pray that as failure produces humility in you, it becomes the soil in which Jesus plants redemptive seeds of growth.

SIX

REWARDS OUR OBEDIENCE

If you love me, you will obey what I command.

☐ **GATHERING TO LISTEN**

At the lunch table at work, people begin making comments about a supervisor. The remarks are mostly critical. "She's demanding and moody sometimes." Another says, "It sure would be great if she would notice my work!" "I don't like the way she runs a meeting—and we never end on time."

You decide to add some comments of your own. "I like Linda, and I admire her business experience," you say. "I also think her ideas for marketing the new product line are creative and profitable. And I must admit I really respect her as a leader in this company."

"You must be kidding," says a coworker. "You *respect* her? How can you say that? You have not done one thing she asked this week. Your report was late, you missed the sales meeting she wanted you to attend, and then you totally ignored her request for more data on the Simmons project. I can't believe you still have a job!"

- In the situation above, imagine that you are the supervisor. What would you do if an employee failed so flagrantly to follow your directions?

☐ ENCOUNTERING JESUS

We might never think of offending a supervisor by repeatedly disobeying him or her. But we often ignore the commands of Jesus and sometimes intentionally disobey them. Yet Jesus teaches that obedience to him and love for him are closely related. And, when practiced, they are rewarded in a rather amazing way.

Read John 14:15-24.

1. What is the relationship between obedience and love as Jesus defines them?

2. Each of the words below can been used to describe the relationship among Jesus, the Father and the Holy Spirit. Which of these elements of this triune relationship impresses you most? Why?

- personal
- intimate
- interdependent
- mysterious
- mutual
- loving

3. In what way is Jesus revealing himself to his followers?

   How is this different from the way he shows himself to the rest of the world?

4. Jesus asks the Father to send a Counselor, the Spirit of truth. What reasons does he give?

   Why is this so important for the lives of his followers?

☐ **JOINING THE CONVERSATION**

5. Jesus makes several statements (and promises) about the presence of God in the life of those who love him. Identify these promises and their impact on your understanding of God.

6. Jesus rewards obedient followers by revealing his love to them and sharing his life with them. That sounds great. So why do we disobey his teaching so often?

☐ **CONNECTING OUR STORIES**

7. In what ways has the Spirit of God been at work in your life this past week?

Is his presence a reality to you?

8. When you realize you have disobeyed the clear teachings of Jesus, what emotions rise within you? For example, do you feel sad, angry, indifferent, frustrated, overwhelmed, depressed or something else?

9. For a few minutes, get into groups of two or three. Choose one statement below and finish it.

   • Without the love and presence of God in my life, I would . . .

   • I do not sense God is present in me because . . .

   • I am struggling to obey the teaching of Jesus because he is asking
     me to . . .

   • I have renewed confidence in God's presence in me because . . .

☐ FINDING OUR WAY

10. The abiding presence of God—Father, Son and Spirit—is a reality for
    those who love and obey Christ. How do we practice this as a com-
    munity of faith?

☐ PRAYING TOGETHER

Believers in Jesus often pray, "Please be with us, God," yet in a real sense
he already is. We desire more intimacy with him, but that doesn't simply
come through prayer; it comes through obedience.

Take time to pray for one another: to understand what Jesus commands, to develop a deeper love for him and to express that love in action.

One way to shape your heart is to pray Scripture. Consider praying through parts of Psalm 119 (it is a long psalm!). The writer has a deep love for God and his commands. You can read or paraphrase these words, meditating on them so that they begin to take root in your heart.

NOTES FOR LEADERS

Each session has a similar format using the components below. Here is a very rough guide for the amount of time you might spend on each segment for a ninety-minute meeting time, excluding additional social time. This is a general guide, and you will learn to adjust the format as you become comfortable working together as a group:

Gathering to Listen	5-10 minutes
Encountering Jesus	15 minutes
Joining the Conversation	20 minutes
Connecting Our Stories	20 minutes
Finding Our Way	10 minutes
Praying Together	about 10 minutes

You can take some shortcuts or take longer as the group decides, but strive to stay on schedule for a ninety-minute meeting including prayer time. You will also want to save time to attend to personal needs and prayer. This will vary by group and can also be accomplished in personal relationships you develop between meetings.

As group leader, know that you help create an environment for spiritual growth. Here are a few things to consider as you invite people to follow in the company of Jesus.

LEADER TIPS

Practice authenticity and truth telling. Do not pretend an elephant is not sitting in the middle of the room when everyone knows it is.

- Does your group have a commitment to pursue personal change and growth?
- Set some ground rules or a covenant for group interactions. Consider values like confidentiality, respect and integrity.
- Model and encourage healthy self-disclosure through icebreakers, storytelling and getting to know one another between meetings.

CONNECTING SEEKERS TO JESUS

This simple process is designed to help you guide a person toward commitment to Christ. It is only a guide, intended to give you the feel of a conversation you might have.

1. Describe what you see going on. "Mike, I sense you are open to knowing Jesus more personally. Is this the case?"

2. Affirm that Jesus is always inviting people to follow him (John 6:35-40). "Mike, Jesus has opened the door to a full and dynamic relationship with him. All who believe in Jesus are welcome. Do you want to place your trust in Jesus?"

3. Describe how sin has separated us from God, making a relationship with God impossible (Romans 3:21-26). "Though Jesus desires fellowship with us, our sin stands in the way. So Jesus went to the cross to pay for that sin, to take away the guilt of that sin and to make reconciliation with God possible again. Are you aware that your sin has become a barrier between you and Jesus?"

4. Show how Jesus' death on the cross bridged the gap between us and God (Romans 5:1-11). "Now we can have peace with God, a relationship with Jesus, because his death canceled out our sin debt. All our offenses against God are taken away by Jesus."

5. Invite them to have a brief conversation with God (2 Corinthians 5:11—6:2). "By asking for his forgiveness and being reconnected to Jesus, we can have new life, one that starts now. Jesus invites you to join him in this new life—to love him, learn his ways, connect to his people and trust in his purposes. We can talk to him now and express that desire if you want to."

These five suggestions are designed to create a dialogue and discern if a person wants to follow Jesus. Points to remember:

1. Keep dialogue authentic and conversational.
2. God is at work here—you are simply a guide, leading someone toward a step of faith in Jesus.
3. The heart is more important than the specific words.
4. People will not understand all that Christ has done, so don't try to confuse them with too much information.
5. Keep it simple.
6. Don't put words in someone's mouth. Let them describe how they want to follow Jesus and participate in his life.

7. Use Scripture as needed. You may recite some or let them read the passages.

8. Remember, this is not a decision to join an organization. It is a relationship with a person, an invitation to a new life and a new community: "Come follow me."

As the person expresses the desire to follow Jesus, encourage them to read the Gospel of Mark and discover the life of Jesus and his teachings more clearly.

SESSION 1.
JESUS RELEASES OUR STRENGTHS.
Luke 9:1-6.

Gathering to Listen (10 minutes). It is important to tap into people's experiences here, but do not let this become a gripe session about others. The point is, "How does it make you feel when your strengths are ignored?"

Encountering Jesus (15 minutes). Jesus is delegating power to his followers. Several have been fishermen, and Jesus knows they have a knack for catching things. Now he wants them to catch people—something that may be outside their comfort zone. He wants them to learn some new skills even as they try to use the strengths he has already endowed them with. But there is a condition, as it were. It is his power and authority—not their own cleverness or abilities—that will make them successful.

He is sending them into a spiritual battle, one that requires spiritual resources. They are called to preach, heal the sick, cure diseases and drive out demons. This is new territory for them, and he wants them to depend totally on him.

This does not mean he neglects or dismisses their strengths. Peter is a rambunctious and impulsive idealist whom Jesus turns into a visionary. His personality and core strengths do not change. Instead, God releases them and empowers him to discover new gifts as well. Later, Paul is a learned Jew and Pharisee, and God takes those strengths and empowers them for greater purposes. Priscilla and Aquila run a business together (Acts 18); then God gets hold of them (through Paul), and soon they are leading house churches together. Apollos is a well-educated communicator, and the power of God turns him into a great evangelist.

Jesus wants us to depend on him for our power. Prayer and trust are key ingredients for the work of ministry. Initially Jesus asks the disciples to take no provisions along so that they will learn to depend on him and on the community of faith for support. In this way, they can point only to God as the reason for their success.

Rejection should be taken as a rejection of Jesus and his words, and the shaking of dust is symbolic, indicating that God will judge those who have rejected his Son (see Luke 10:13-15). Enduring persecution and rejection is part of being a disciple of Jesus (see John 15:18-25).

Joining the Conversation (20 minutes). These questions are designed to help members compare their personal experience as followers of Jesus (or even as those seeking to understand who he is) with that of the disciples. We too are given power. But we are not the Twelve. Our mission is similar, but our context is different. The power we have is just as dynamic, but a special portion was allotted to the Twelve for their initial work of authenticating the message of Messiah.

There is always debate within and between churches as to whether every Christian should be casting out demons, raising the dead, healing the sick and so on. It is true that at times our lack of faith may be one reason for our failure to see God's power at work in our midst (Matthew 13:58 and Luke 8:48 are examples). Yet it is clear that working of miracles and other gifts are not given to all (1 Corinthians 12:9-10).

The focus here is not what the disciples are doing—the power and the results. The focus is the *source* of the power and authority. God handles the results. Do we understand that we have in Christ this power to act on his behalf, pray bold prayers, believe the unbelievable and accomplish the inconceivable? God gives certain powers for certain situations, as he wills. If the Twelve had already been given power to preach at this point, why did Jesus later tell them to wait for the Holy Spirit to come so they would have power to be his witnesses (Acts 1:8)? We must be careful when seeking to make universal application of Scripture that may have been intended for a specific situation or audience. Some great followers of Jesus and teachers of the gospel (like Timothy, Apollos, Priscilla, Aquila, Mary Magdalene, Martha and others) are not said to have performed any miracles; nonetheless, they were given great power and had life-changing ministries for Christ.

Connecting Our Stories (20 minutes). Help members understand that they have the opportunity to be vessels of God's power as Jesus releases their strengths. Allow time for people to express expectations, frustrations, hopes, failures or inadequacies. Each experience is different. But we want to encourage each other to see things anew. Power comes in many forms—the power to heal a relationship, the power to forgive someone who has made an unjust accusation, the power to share the love of Christ with a friend. We are uniquely gifted and empowered, but we are not alone. Followers of Christ form a body, a community that together longs to have God work through them.

Finding Our Way (10 minutes). Take time to encourage one another here. Explore ways to discover strengths and gifts. If your church has a spiritual gift assessment or affirmation process (like the Willow Creek *Network* curriculum), encourage people to enter that process. Members of the group can affirm the strengths they see in one another as well.

Praying Together (10 minutes). Don't be afraid to pray boldly. Bold prayers do not have to sound like spiritual hype; there is no need to be loud or flamboyant in order to be sincere and dependent on God. The key is a humble heart and open hands. Ask God for power, and remember the authority that followers of Jesus have to live and minister in his name.

SESSION 2.
JESUS ALIGNS OUR VISION.
Matthew 7:1-5.

Gathering to Listen (10 minutes). This is designed to help people realize that we all have blind spots—not just in our vision but in our thinking. This "icebreaker" should open people up to the need for vision clarity. Use it as a bridge builder.

Encountering Jesus (15 minutes). The follower of Christ who judges others usurps the role of God. It is not our place to condemn or to pass judgment. But we are called to be discerning and wise (see Romans 14:10-13; 1 Corinthians 5:5; Galatians 1:8-9; 6:1; Philippians 3:2, 15). And so we make judgments (discerning assessments) without passing judgment (a hypocritical condemnation) on others.

Jesus uses a rather humorous image of a person with a huge log or plank in their eye trying to spot a small speck of debris in another's eye. So it is with those who judge hypocritically. We must first deal with our own sin and shortcomings before condemning the same behavior in others. Imagine a doctor who is one hundred pounds overweight condemning you for not exercising enough, or a parent who spends every afternoon at the local casino telling a daughter not to buy a lottery ticket because it is a waste of money.

Jesus wants to shape a spirit of humility and dependence in his followers and protect them from arrogant, judgmental attitudes that would weaken the force and integrity of the gospel.

Joining the Conversation (20 minutes). These questions will require members to be reflective and introspective—to examine themselves in light of the truth. This will likely be uncomfortable and awkward if your group is new to this type of thing. So be discerning as to how much you push and probe.

It is often wise to do this kind of activity in subgroups of two or three people. Thus people can take some risks and speak openly with just a few others. The point is to develop trust and to build a community of mutual concern and support. We all have logs in our eye—and most people know what they are if they spend much time around us.

This sharing and discussion will help prepare people for the prayer time as they begin to look at areas of their life where they need to grow and mature.

Connecting Our Stories (20 minutes). Much of the world sees the institutional church as hypocritical, rarely practicing what it preaches. If the shoe fits, we must wear it. It is important to change this perception and the reality behind it, not because it will make us feel better but because it will remove unnecessary barriers to the message of the gospel.

Admission of weakness, sin and guilt is a sign of strength and maturity in a follower of Jesus. Repentance—changing our patterns and thoughts so they begin to conform to the life of Jesus—is a daily task, not a onetime event. We truly need a conversion, a change in the way we approach relationships and decisions. So help members envision not an ideal church but a truthful and honest church. And that begins with individual Christians. Since our sanctification is a process, we should admit that sometimes we move three steps forward and two steps back.

Finding Our Way (10 minutes). It is important that we in the body of Christ look out for one another. To correct or "admonish" one another is a function of those who live in the company of Jesus (Colossians 3:16; 1 Thessalonians 5:12). But it must be done with grace, humility, an attitude of self-examination and the goal of helping one another mature. It is not done for faultfinding or to make one feel superior to another. That is legalism and the worst sort of hypocrisy.

Remind members of the spirit that must underlie such correction. Ask plainly, "How can we help each other live God-honoring lives?" Do not shrink back from the truth. Judgment (correction, evaluation and so on) begins with the family of God, according to 1 Peter 4:17. So we do business with God first at the personal level, then at the communal level. It is God's job to judge the world, not ours. Even Jesus did not come to pass judgment on earth (John 3:16-21). It is the Father who gives him the authority to judge those who have rejected his love and message of reconciliation, a judgment that will come later (read John 5:16-27 and 2 Corinthians 5:10).

Praying Together (10 minutes). This can be a great time of affirmation and encouragement. Prayers may be directed toward spiritual growth and overcoming sin in the power of community. Will you be courageous enough to do the work of discipleship together—with God's help?

SESSION 3.
JESUS DEMANDS OUR DEVOTION.
Luke 14:25-35.

Gathering to Listen (10 minutes). This opening story addresses the tension that may arise from the title of this session, "Jesus Demands Our Devotion." To think of Jesus as "demanding" sounds so negative, so oppressive. We want to make the distinction between an attitude (being demanding) and an action (making a demand or challenging someone to a higher level of performance or character).

Encountering Jesus (15 minutes). Jesus makes some strong demands on his followers. The difference is that he leads the way. He has given up his family, his career, his comfort, his stature (see Philippians 2) and eventually his life. He is the first to pick up the cross of discipleship. He has no place to lay his head and has already demonstrated a life of faith and integrity.

Jesus wants supreme devotion and commitment from followers. It is not at all a hypocritical request from One who is about to make the supreme sacrifice on the cross of Calvary. He asks us to yield ownership and rights, not necessarily to throw everything away. All we have must be subjected to his will and his call on our life, even the close ties of family.

To take up the cross was a sign of full commitment: for the one headed for a crucifixion in Jesus' day there was no going back. One never returned from a crucifixion. Jesus used this image to help us see that we must put to death all that would distract us from following him. In Luke 9:57-62 Jesus already laid out the level of commitment he expected and clarified the focus of our allegiances and priorities. As Dietrich Bonhoeffer said, "When Jesus calls a man [or woman], he bids him [her] come and die." It is not a very pleasant image, and Jesus intended it to be disconcerting.

In each illustration of counting the cost, Jesus refers to something that is difficult to stop or to start over. To build a building you must secure land, hire workers and purchase materials. Once the project is under way, it would be hard to simply start over again. You are fully committed. Such is the case with battle as well. In the middle of a military engagement, a commander cannot say, "On second thought, let's not fight these people—I've changed my mind." In each case the initial decision must be carefully weighed because the consequences are significant and failure is final.

And so the potential follower considers what it means to give it all up for Jesus. This is no small decision. Even as we explain God's grace in the gospel to others, we must remember his expectations for the life that we are called to live. Grace may be free, but it is not cheap.

Once committed to following, we are to be like good salt—salt that has taste. When you put salt on food, its effect is noticeable. Otherwise salt would be useless. So would be the disciple who has no impact or influence for Jesus.

Joining the Conversation (20 minutes). There is no need to be harsh or pushy here, just to be sober and recognize that there are costs to a life lived in Christ. To identify with him is to identify not only with his love, grace and power but also with his suffering, self-denial and death (Romans 6).

Help members begin to look inside, consider their commitments and reflect on their relationship to Jesus.

Connecting Our Stories (20 minutes). Self-denial sounds like a waste of time in a culture filled with many options and choices targeted at our self-fulfillment. You will find many titles in the "Self-Help" section of a bookstore, but you would be hard pressed to find the "Self-Denial" section, or many books that take up this topic.

Giving up our primary allegiance to parents, surrendering our life to Christ and committing ourselves daily to a life of self-sacrifice is so countercultural (especially to Asian and African cultures) that many will think we are strange. Allegiance and loyalty to family is paramount in many cultures outside the United States. In most cases, though, leaving family is always hard. But in doing so we join the company of many who have gone before us in the name of Jesus.

Finding Our Way (10 minutes). Ask members to do a practical assessment of what matters most to them. Perhaps people could write down their thoughts privately. What would it look like to place those things under the leadership of Jesus? What would the results be? What kind of life would that mean? What kind of rewards can we expect?

Praying Together (10 minutes). Romans 12:9-21 is a wonderful text for prayer and personal evaluation. But it is written to a church—a community. So look at it as a group and ask how God might make your group a place where this way of life is expressed and practiced.

SESSION 4.
JESUS EXPECTS OUR BEST.
Matthew 25:14-30.

Gathering to Listen (10 minutes). As members reflect on what it means to give their best, see if you notice the difference between perfectionism and excellence. Don't be surprised if people bring this up (hard work versus workaholic tendencies, etc.). Stay on purpose. Focus on how it makes people feel and what sacrifices it requires. This should be a good initial discussion, especially after completing "Jesus Demands Our Devotion" at the last gathering.

Encountering Jesus (15 minutes). This parable follows three others Jesus has told (Matthew 24:42—25:13). Each of the others has to do with readiness and preparedness for the master's arrival. In this case, several servants are expected to produce a return on the investment the master has entrusted to each of them.

Each servant (or slave) is given an amount according to his ability; thus, each is capable of managing the initial sum. A talent was a large unit of measure for gold, silver and copper, and calculating the exact amounts in today's dollars is almost impossible. What is more important is the relative amount of money each received. In each case, however, it was a sizable amount.

Instead of "Well done," the third servant-investor hears a strong rebuke and receives a stiff judgment from the master, casting him into the darkness. He is called "wicked and lazy," which gives us an idea of what the master had expected. He is not called a poor manager, nor is he the victim of an economic downturn. He is called lazy because stewarding resources wisely takes planning and effort and he had avoided this. And he is evil because he has harbored resentment and condemnation toward the master and has disobeyed his instructions.

Joining the Conversation (20 minutes). The parable has many features, but what generates the most discussion is whether the master is meant to symbolize God—and if so, will God act like this master? To some degree, God does act this way. Our actions have consequences. God has given us so much (gifts, salvation, freedom), and to waste it is a bit of a slap in his face.

But we must be careful when interpreting a parable. We cannot press the analogy too far. This parable is not designed to give a full picture of the actions of God. Rather, it dramatically teaches how foolish it is to waste what we have been given and to be unfaithful toward God. Like a good parent, God brings judgment for rebellion against him. Therefore, we must be sober about the consequences for rejecting the love, teaching, grace and good gifts of God.

The main point of the parable, however, is that watchfulness (the theme of all these parables) should characterize the disciples of Jesus. In this case, productivity is expected in accordance with what measure of resources and abilities God has given us.

The clear message is how angry the master is with a manager who has been given much but has done so little with it. Like this master, God is coming back to judge the works of his servants, and it will be a sad day for those who have done nothing but bury them. "Weeping and gnashing of teeth" implies deep regret and anguish over opportunities squandered. Such servants cannot remain in the presence of the master. Perhaps the irresponsible servant thought he could wait and do something later because the master would be gone a long time. But the previous parables remind us that Jesus may return unexpectedly, and happy will be the servant who is about the work of the kingdom when he returns.

Connecting Our Stories (20 minutes). This parable, like all parables, must be interpreted with focus on the main point. Specific interpretation of minor details in the parable is unwise, for it can stretch the plain meaning and emphasis of the story. (There is no need here, for example, to argue over whether these servants are believers or unbelievers or whether this is the final judgment. The point is a servant's lack of effort which results in rejection, tears and regret. Whether Jesus is speaking specifically about what hell is like is debated by scholars and not necessary for the reader to know to make the parable powerful.)

Kingdom life requires faithfulness and watchfulness. Jesus wants listeners to understand the consequences of our actions and what he expects—that we give God the best effort we can with what he has given us to use.

Finding Our Way (10 minutes). It is important for all of us identify the gifts, talents and abilities we have. What would it look like if everyone used these fully? How might lives around us be affected if we made the effort to be involved in the activities and ways of Jesus?

Legalism always produces death. There is a crucial difference between making an effort and striving for perfection. God does not want us to worry about whether we have done enough; he wants us to work hard with a view toward pleasing him. If we do, we will not be disappointed when he arrives to settle accounts.

Does the group need to be challenged or reminded of these realities?

Praying Together (10 minutes). Pray that God will help you avoid sloth and wastefulness. Are there members of the group who are not putting gifts and abilities to use wisely? Pray that the Holy Spirit would speak to each one and help them see what is being neglected or wasted. Pray that we would all give our best—best time, talents and treasure—to the Master.

SESSION 5.
JESUS REDEEMS OUR FAILURES.
Mark 14:29-31, 44-52, 66-72.

Gathering to Listen (10 minutes). Generally this will be a fun, light discussion. The topic is a hard one because it concerns failure. So this opening story is designed to break the ice a bit before dealing with our failures in honest, redemptive ways.

Encountering Jesus (15 minutes). Jesus gives his followers three truths here: he will rise from the dead, the disciples will all desert him, and he will be in Galilee after the resurrection. Interestingly, Peter does not react to the resurrection prediction, which implies that a death will take place. Instead he reacts to the statement about "falling away" and assures Christ that *he* will not.

Peter acts on his own but in some ways represents all the disciples. Everyone is quick to declare their allegiance, but Jesus knows their weaknesses and their imminent betrayal.

Judas is called "one of the twelve" here by Mark, as if to remind the reader that he is part of the inner circle, has seen the miracles and love of Christ firsthand, and yet devises the betrayal scheme.

Each of us feels great sadness and sometimes anger when friends or family turn their backs on us. Jesus certainly felt grief and sadness when his closest disciples ran from him, denied him or outright betrayed him.

The teaching and healing ministry of Jesus has been on display for everyone to see. He has acted openly and with integrity, fulfilling the law and remaining above reproach. He challenges his accusers to provide a basis for his arrest. At the same time, he acknowledges biblical prophecy and understands these actions as the fulfillment of these prophecies. He is not surprised and knows that his hour has come. Jesus is fully submissive to the Father; he leads no rebellion against the authorities nor against his Father in heaven.

Jesus is betrayed with a kiss, usually given as a greeting of friendship and respect in the ancient Middle East. Rabbis were greeted by their disciples with a kiss. This action therefore is a great irony. You would respect a rebel to simply point to Jesus and say, "There he is!" A kiss is an even more shameful act.

As to the young man who fled the scene naked, scholars believe it was Mark himself, the Gospel writer. Only he records the episode. Usually people wore two garments, an inner and outer garment. But Mark had only the outer garment, and it was made of linen instead of wool, which suggest that he was wealthy. Perhaps he had gotten wind of the events that were about to take place and had dressed quickly, rushing out in the night to see what might happen. "Perhaps the main point of the story," comments Walter Wessel, "and the reason Mark included it, was to show that the forsakenness of Jesus was total. Even this youth forsook him" ("Mark," in *Expositor's Bible Commentary*).

Joining the Conversation (20 minutes). Human nature is tainted by sin. We are depraved. Every part of us has been affected by sin and the brokenness that results. We are weak and prone to rebellion, denial and self-preservation.

Betrayal and desertion produce feelings of anger, shame and unworthiness. Children of divorce and spouses alike often blame themselves for a marital breakup, even if their contribution to the problems was minimal. When something bad happens, we are prone to assume that we are bad people. But Jesus understood that his rejection was part of the Father's plan to secure redemption for all people (Isaiah 53:12; Zechariah 13:7).

The soldiers and religious leaders came to take Jesus away at night to avoid a scene and forestall the possibility of a revolt by the crowds who loved him and followed him everywhere.

In Mark 14:71 Peter is feeling the guilt of his actions. He has been following at a distance, like Adam and Eve, who hid themselves after their rebellion (something we are all apt to do when we have offended or ignored God). Confronted by a servant girl twice, then by others who also suspect he is a disciple of Jesus, Peter goes into a rage, calling down curses on himself. This is like saying today, "I swear on my life I had nothing to do with it!" In effect, "May I be cursed if this is true!" The enraged, defensive response simply exposes his guilt.

But this anger and frustration at being identified give way to utter sadness and grief when he hears the rooster crow. Peter is crushed, broken and devastated at what he has done. We do not see this in the other disciples who deserted Jesus (the text simply does not tell us). Though Judas is ashamed and despondent, he is never repentant like Peter. There is a difference between saying, "I am sad for what I did because it makes me feel bad," and "I am sad for what I did because it hurts you and I am sorry."

Connecting Our Stories (20 minutes). As members recount stories of failure or relational breakdown, remind them that Jesus can redeem the past and restore us after we fail, as he did with Peter. With Jesus, failure is never final unless, like Judas Iscariot, we choose that it be so. Some may argue that Judas could not have helped what he did because Scripture had predicted that someone would betray Jesus. God is sovereign, but we have choices. His sovereignty—his oversight of all things and people—does not mean we are puppets. Under God's control we are free to act, but we often act according to our sin nature when we don't let the Holy Spirit guide us. That God knows us and what we will do does not alleviate our responsibility for our actions. (For more on this, refer members to *Evangelism and the Sovereignty of God* by J. I. Packer. He handles this complex issue well.)

Finding Our Way (10 minutes). Help members rediscover their worth and usefulness in the eyes of Jesus. People may not want to talk about their failures—and that is not the point. The point is to help them gain new perspective on failure in light of how Jesus has treated Peter and others. Remind them also of Jonah, David, Abraham, Moses, Jacob, Rahab (the harlot) and other Old Testament figures who submitted their lives—and thus their shortcomings—to God and watched him use them for his glory.

Praying Together (10 minutes). This is an opportunity to bring great encouragement, healing, hope and vision. You may want to ask members to write for a few minutes and dream of how God might use them in spite of their past mistakes. It may be helpful to share your own thoughts first. Keep it brief. "I believe God can use me to . . ." would be a way to approach this. Then pray for one another, asking God to show you his power and affirmation as you take steps of faith. It takes faith to believe that God sees us better than we see ourselves.

SESSION 6.
JESUS REWARDS OUR OBEDIENCE.
John 14:15-24.

Gathering to Listen (10 minutes). The work world is often brutal, and relationships are easily damaged. Respect, authority, submission, loyalty and performance are all mixed together. What people think of us at work affects how we relate to them. This has application to the spiritual life as well. Help members see that relationships (good or bad) affect how we view authority.

Encountering Jesus (15 minutes). There is a difference here between obeying someone to earn their love or respect and obeying someone because you love them or respect them. Jesus is talking about the latter. It is natural for Jesus lovers to be Jesus followers—in word and actions.

Jesus describes a very close relationship within the Trinity. All the words listed can be used to describe it in some way. Members may be particularly impressed with one or two of them. Notice the following:

- Personal: the persons of the Trinity (though each is fully God), and their relationship is personal.
- Intimate:
    the Spirit lives in the believer (verse 17)
    the Son is in the Father (verse 20)
    the Son is in us (verse 20)
    we are in the Son (verse 20)
- Interdependent: the Son asks the Father to send the Spirit (verse 16).
- Mysterious: somehow the Father and Son make their home in us (verse 23).
- Mutual: the entire Trinity is at work here in the believer (verses 16, 20).
- Loving: Jesus and the Father both express love to followers (verses 21, 23).

If we put all this together, we see that the Spirit is the active and personal presence and power of the Father and Son in the believer. Through the Spirit, the believer is said to be in Christ, and Christ is also in us; the Spirit is in us, and the Father has made his home in us. (See Romans 8:10-11; 2 Corinthians 5:17; Colossians 1:27; use these verses as needed during the group discussion.)

To the world Jesus shows his glory and provides miracles and teaching. He has shown the world what the Father looks like (John 14:9-10). But Jesus reveals himself uniquely to his followers by taking up residency in us—he abides in us (John 15:4-11). This is one of the great mysteries of our relationship with Jesus Christ. Theologians call this "union with Christ," a deep intimacy and participation in his life.

The Holy Spirit is called "the Spirit of Christ" and the "Spirit of God" in Romans 8:9. The Bible uses these terms to mean the same person. The Spirit is further called our Comforter, Advocate or Counselor. He is our representative and guide, the One who connects us with God and glorifies the risen Christ.

It is difficult to love and obey Jesus on our own power. This is one reason he has sent the Spirit. When Jesus was on earth he could be physically present with only a few. Now, in the Holy Spirit, he is present in every believer providing guidance and power so we can obey Christ.

Joining the Conversation (20 minutes). Jesus talks about the presence of God in the life of those who love him.

- The Father will give us the Spirit.
- The Spirit will be with us forever.
- Jesus will not leave us alone.
- Because he lives, we will live.
- We will know and understand that we are in him.
- The Father will love us as we love Christ.
- The Father and Son will live in us.
- The one who does not love Jesus will not be loved by the Father.

This means that the believer has the power and presence of God available at all times, no matter how badly we have failed Jesus (see previous lesson) or how much we need him.

All this may make us wonder why we do not love and obey Jesus more readily than we do now. There are several reasons. Here are a few.

- We need to mature and grow.
- We may not yet know all of Christ's commands.
- We still sin; the sin nature is not fully eradicated.
- We are tempted by the things of this world—power, lust, money.
- Failing to abide in Christ, we lose touch with him.
- We forget that we will give an account for our works here on earth.

Connecting Our Stories (20 minutes). Some members of your group may not understand the role of the Spirit in their life or sense his presence. Others may not be believers. So it is important for believers to explain how they see God at work in them through the Spirit. You may have to lead the way. Let others see how the Spirit works—albeit mysteriously—in very real ways. He is present in relationships, building our character, reminding us of our identity in Christ and our worth as his child, helping us seek God's forgiveness, and giving us assurance that we are free in Christ as we repent and confess sin.

Allow people to express how they feel when they let God down. These emotions are real. Notice how Peter acted. He tried to hide his guilt and ignore the truth. But when we begin to acknowledge that we fail, God can use those emotions of guilt and sadness to draw us back to him. Even anger. We may be furious with ourselves for yielding to a temptation and disobeying Christ. But if we express that and allow the feelings of remorse and process of repentance to follow, Jesus can shape our heart again for his purposes.

People need to be reminded of the "seventy times seven" forgiveness principle in Matthew 18. Jesus continues to forgive. That is what is so amazing about grace. Help members remember this—or understand it for the first time—as they complete the statements in this section. Listen carefully to their hearts and note ways the group can help encourage and support each other in attempts to follow and honor Christ.

Finding Our Way (10 minutes). Sometimes we need to verbalize what we know about Christ. We need to affirm our love for him in prayer and our desire to obey him. That was the idea behind many of the early creeds. Though they affirmed doctrinal truth, the idea was that such statements of truth should remind us of our standing in Christ by faith, what he has done on our behalf, the hope we have in him and the need to follow him with all our heart.

Perhaps it is time for your group to develop a covenant statement or even a brief creed laying out what you believe about God, Jesus, the power of the Spirit and your desire to walk faithfully. Putting some of this in writing together might help you support one another. It will help the group practice what it preaches (1 John 2:6; see *Leading Life-Changing Small Groups* by Bill Donahue [Zondervan] for more on making a covenant).

Praying Together (10 minutes). Praying through parts of Psalm 119 can be a rich experience for the group. Read the psalm ahead of meeting time and choose an appropriate section for your group. Use the short sections shown in your Bible. In the original text, each section was a series of phrases beginning with the same letter of the Hebrew alphabet; verses 1-16 in the Hebrew all begin with an *aleph,* which is like the *A* in our alphabet. Take just one of these sections—some eight to ten verses—and pray it aloud, phrase by phrase. It will help people see how one's love for God begins to mature into a love of his commands and teachings, especially those of Jesus.

Also available from InterVarsity Press and Willow Creek Resources

BIBLE 101. *Where truth meets life.*
Bill Donahue, series editor

The Bible 101 series is designed for those who want to know how to study God's Word, understand it clearly and apply it to their lives in a way that produces personal transformation. Geared especially for groups, the series can also profitably be used for individual study. Each guide has five sessions that overview essential information and teach new study skills. The sixth session brings the skills together in a way that relates them to daily life.

FOUNDATIONS: *How We Got Our Bible*
Bill Donahue

TIMES & PLACES: *Picturing the Events of the Bible*
Michael Redding

COVER TO COVER: *Getting the Bible's Big Picture*
Gerry Mathisen

STUDY METHODS: *Experiencing the Power of God's Word*
Kathy Dice

INTERPRETATION: *Discovering the Bible for Yourself*
Judson Poling

PARABLES & PROPHECY: *Unlocking the Bible's Mysteries*
Bill Donahue

GREAT THEMES: *Understanding the Bible's Core Doctrines*
Michael Redding

PERSONAL DEVOTION: *Taking God's Word to Heart*
Kathy Dice